THE

Sales
Skills

*They Don't Teach
at Business School*

THE

25

Sales
Skills

They Don't Teach at Business School

by

STEPHAN SCHIFFMAN

America's #1 Corporate Sales Trainer

Adams Media Corporation
Avon, Massachusetts

Published by Adams Media, an F+W Publications Company
57 Littlefield Street, Avon, MA 02322. U.S.A.
www.adamsmedia.com

ISBN: 1-58062-614-9

Printed in Canada.

J I H G F E D C

Library of Congress Cataloging-in-Publication Data
Schiffman, Stephan.
25 sales skills they don't teach at business school /
by Stephan Schiffman.
p.   cm.
ISBN 1-58062-614-9
1. Selling. I. Title: Twenty-five sales skills they
don't teach at business school. II. Title: 25 sales skills
they do not teach at business school. III. Title.
HF5438.25.S3333   2002
658.85—dc21   2001055303

This publication is designed to provide accurate and authorita-
tive information with regard to the subject matter covered. It is
sold with the understanding that the publisher is not engaged
in rendering legal, accounting, or other professional advice. If
legal advice or other expert assistance is required, the services
of a competent professional person should be sought.
— From a *Declaration of Principles* jointly adopted
by a Committee of the American Bar Association
and a Committee of Publishers and Associations

Rear cover photograph:
The Ira Rosen Studios, South Bellmore, New York

This book is available at quantity discounts for bulk purchases.
For information, call 1-800-872-5627.

Contents

Introduction: The Hidden Sales Curriculum

Some elements of selling you may learn in a classroom. Others come from experience. In this book, I've tried to incorporate both.

The inspiration for the volume you're holding in your hands arose from a discussion I had with my daughter Jennifer, who recently graduated from college. Jennifer pointed out that certain core skills are part of a standard education—reading and math, for instance—but that the adaptation of those skills to the real world is dependent on another lesson entirely. This informal lesson may be more important than the "nuts and bolts" course of study that must precede it.

A "subject" like learning to order from a menu at a good restaurant isn't specifically covered when we're taught to read. Similarly, no one teaches us how to select a topic of conversation that will open up a group of cautious strangers during those first few strained moments of a party. (Apparently, this type of topic is never covered in courses called "social studies.") These skills, and many others, Jennifer continued, must be acquired by each of us as we go along, out there in the real world.

It occurred to me that much the same thing is true of the world of sales. Certain basic skills are taught—and retaught—to help salespeople expand their contact base, connect the people in that base to various products and services, and increase their income. And yet veteran salespeople possess skills that go beyond this—skills that most new salespeople don't have, skills that training seminars, business school courses, and formal sessions in sales school simply don't cover.

I call this the "hidden curriculum" of the sales world. And I've tried to write about it in this book. This essential curriculum comprises the authentic sales lessons that experienced salespeople always seem to learn from the environment rather than from a business course or training seminar.

Salespeople also learn from one another, of course. Every one of the chapters in this book is based on a question I've received from one of our own salespeople. Since I still sell for a living, I'm able to offer anecdotes and suggestions based on recent experience. What appears on the following pages is, in essence, in answer to the questions that come *after* you implement the good ideas and strategies you learn in a marketing class or sales training seminar.

If you're interested in learning how to have great conversations with prospects virtually every time out, how to spot bad selling advice on the Internet, how to use questions to increase your average value per account, when it makes sense to ask a question you know your prospect can't answer, or why making a mistake in front of a prospect is sometimes the best thing you can do—this book is for you. You won't learn any of this in school—but you will learn about it here.

What follows is some insider advice culled from twenty-seven years of face-to-face selling. You may have to implement the ideas in the main section of this book without the help of an instructor, but once you become familiar with these concepts, my guess is that you'll wonder why they *don't* teach this stuff in sales school.

Until the formal curriculum is updated to reflect something more expansive than the traditional selling admonitions, I hope this book will point you in the right direction.

Stephan Schiffman
New York, NY
January, 2001

Beware of Bad Advice on the Internet

How much should I trust what I read
on the Internet about sales?

———————

The Internet has changed the way many people sell. Few of us could have imagined, six or
seven years ago, how easy it would become to
gain access to some of the most vital daily
selling information. Researching a company?
You can now check for its Web site easily.
Hungry for new leads? Dozens of online
resources can point you toward new people
and companies to contact. Looking for advice
on how to improve your selling technique?
Hundreds of (self-appointed) sales experts are

———————

only a click away.

And this is where you can get yourself into trouble. Too many sales "gurus" use their sites to dispense advice that can sabotage the job of building a relationship with your prospect. Consider the following:

Bad advice: Don't work with the prospect to develop a plan that "makes sense"—instead, use pressure tactics. A site we visited encouraged salespeople to ask this question when face to face with a hesitant contact: "Now, don't you agree that this product can help you or would be of benefit to you?" Ouch. A better approach would be to ask, "What exactly are you trying to get accomplished in this area?"

Bad advice: Find the pain. Several sites we encountered advised salespeople to use questions to plant subliminal "hints" designed to get prospects to reveal that they actually hate their current vendor. Examples: "Do you also worry about . . . ?" "How tough a position does that put you in?" Instead of trying to find the pain—which may or may not exist—salespeople should focus on finding out what the prospect actually *does*.

Bad advice: "Always be closing." This outdated maxim showed up as constructive advice on more than one of the sales sites we visited, as did any number of manipulative closing "tricks" that will quickly destroy emerging relationships. More pragmatic advice: "Always be asking questions." At the conclusion of an in-depth information-gathering period—which should occupy 75 percent of any sales process—you can present a plan that makes sense to the other person, and close by asking, "It makes sense to me—what do you think?"

THE BOTTOM LINE: It's too easy to set up a Web site—which makes it hard to find a good one with relevant, responsible information for salespeople. Beware of the advice you take from the Internet.

Use Company Events to Move the Relationship Forward

"I've lost ground with a couple of former prospects who asked me to 'keep in touch' the last time I spoke to them. I want to win some *action* in these relationships after a few dormant weeks (or months!). How do I do it?"

——————

"Thanks for calling to confirm—but I'm afraid I'm going to have to cancel our meeting for next week. We've decided to put a hold on all our spending in this area for now. We'll be reevaluating in a couple of months. Keep in touch, all right?"

It's part of the sales landscape—a law as dependable as gravity. No matter how effective, persuasive, or experienced a given salesperson is, some percentage of that person's promising leads will turn into "opportunities." These are static contacts that aren't moving through the sales process and can't be counted on to provide income—at least for the time being.

The question really isn't whether contacts will fall into the "opportunity" category but what steps to take when they do. How do you reignite interest and generate activity within your list of "cold" prospects? Canadian sales representative Gino Sette came up with an interesting strategy.

Gino decided to write a letter to every prospect who had decided *not* to buy from him over a given period. Basically, the letter said this: "It was a pleasure meeting with you a while back to talk about what your company was doing. Even though we were unable to move forward at that time, I'm still thinking about you."

Gino then invited each "cold" contact to sit in at one of his company's upcoming events. "This will give you an opportunity to evaluate, firsthand how applicable what we do is to your business environment," he wrote. "Attached is a list of all upcoming training where my clients have approved outside observers. I've also included a brief description of each of the programs."

According to Gino, he got calls from prospects who were very interested in observing specific programs, even though they had initially declined his firm's services.

The letter-writing strategy had another application as well. Gino decided to write to each member of his active client base and extend the same invitation. The letter began as follows: "First of all, let me thank you for allowing us to work with you and XYZ Company. We are very excited to have you as part of our client list, as you are a significant player. It is for this reason that I would like to extend the following invitation to you . . ."

As his flurry of return calls proved, Gino's innovative letter technique is an effective way to win back (or solidify) your position on the to-do lists of your customers and inactive leads. His idea can be adapted to training programs, open houses, media events, and any number of other occasions.

THE BOTTOM LINE: Send your "cold" leads—and your customers—invitations to upcoming company events.

Stop Spinning Your Wheels with People Who Don't Really Want to Work with You—and Start "Following the Yes"

"I'm spending too much time with leads that don't seem to turn into anything. How can I tell who's *really* interested in working with my organization?"

First and foremost, let's define what we mean by "prospect." A prospect is someone who is willing to take an *active* step—demonstrated by a specific time commitment—to talk seriously about the possibility of working with you.

That's an extremely important definition. Do yourself—and your career—a favor: Commit it to memory!

The most effective salespeople learn to spot people who aren't giving them a clear "yes" answer to follow, and distinguish those people from the rest of the world. The trick is to understand that the relevant "yes" answers take many important forms *before* the close, but virtually *always* include some kind of time commitment:

"Yes, I'll meet with you next Tuesday at three o'clock."

"Yes, I'll introduce you to my boss next Monday morning."

"Yes, I'll take a look at your notes and tell you what works and what doesn't. Let's schedule a conference call."

"Yes, I'll schedule a meeting with the full committee. When are you free?"

"Yes, we'd like you to start on January first."

No book can teach you how to make a prospect do something he or she doesn't want to do. If you follow the advice that appears below, however, you *will* make the most of your time and maximize the number of prospects who decide to tell *you* what to do—by giving you business.

THREE STEPS TO FOLLOWING THE YES

Here are the three steps you can take right now to begin *following the yes*.

Step One

Make a habit of "throwing out the ball" (suggesting a Next step) to a number of people each and every day.

If you're uncertain what your target number should be, read *Cold Calling Techniques (That Really Work!)* or take D.E.I.'s course in appointment making. Either way, you'll work through the numbers thoroughly to set your daily prospecting goals. ("Throwing out the ball" might sound like this: "I'd love to get together with you to talk about what we've done with the XYZ Company. Can we meet Tuesday at three o'clock at your office?")

(By the way, if you're interested in taking advantage of on-line courses in Appointment Making, Prospect Management, or High Efficiency Selling, you can find out more about those training resources at *www.dei-*

sales.com. Our Web site offers full-scale on-line overviews of all of our in-person training programs.)

Step Two

Learn to distinguish "sounds like YES" answers from "actual YES" answers.

"Actual YES" answers are ones in which the person agrees to a clear next step with you, complete with date and time, that's scheduled for the near future (typically, within the next two weeks). "Actual YES" answers could sound like this:

You:	Can we get together Wednesday at two o'clock to talk about this further?
Prospect:	Wednesday's no good for me; what about Friday morning?

Or they could sound like this:

You:	Why don't you and I meet with your supplier next week to set up a plan?
Prospect:	You know what? That's a great idea. When are you free?

Step Three

Treat everything that's not an "actual YES" as though it were an "actual NO."

Here's the really critical point: *Stop wasting time with people who are not actually moving through the sales process with you.* So even if the person says, "Call me sometime next month," we put that person *lower* on the priority list than someone who says, "Let's talk next Monday at two o'clock."

THE BOTTOM LINE: Invest your time wisely, move on to someone new, and stop spinning your wheels.

Harness the Power of "I Didn't Anticipate That"

> "I just had the worst meeting of my life.
> I had no idea what to say when the
> prospect shot me down. What do you
> do in a situation like that?"

The most successful salespeople work from the principle that *all responses are anticipated*. What does that mean? It means that, as professionals, we've had enough conversations with enough people over the years to develop a reliable sense of what's likely to happen next during an exchange with a prospect or customer. Put more bluntly, experienced salespeople don't get taken by surprise all that often. If that's a fact of sales life—and it is—

we can actually use this principle to our advantage in turning around the negative responses we hear.

Consider the following scenario. Alan, a young sales representative in the telecommunications industry, meets with Bill, a middle-aged MIS director at a *Fortune* 100 company. At the end of a good first meeting, Alan says to the prospect, "I'd like to get together with you again so I can show you a preliminary proposal—an outline of what we might be able to do for you. Why don't we set a meeting for next Tuesday at three o'clock?" And then the roof seems to fall in.

"Alan," Bill says, "it's been nice talking to you, and you're certainly working on some interesting projects, but let me save us both some time. I've been in charge of telecom here for fifteen years, and I have a pretty good idea of what your company has to offer. I really don't think there's a match here. But if you want to, you can go ahead and mail your information to me, and I'll call you back if I'm interested. "

Suppose Alan were to try to explain *why* what he wanted to outline in the preliminary proposal would be perfect for Bill's organization? How would that go over? More than likely, Bill would get annoyed. He might even suggest that Alan do a little more homework about his industry before attempting to continue the conversation. But consider another approach, one that emphasizes Alan's experience in the world of sales, levels the playing field, and points the relationship in a positive direction.

Suppose that, when Bill puts up a roadblock by saying something like, "Go ahead and mail the information to me instead," Alan looks a little startled. There's a brief pause. Then Alan says, *"Gee, I really didn't anticipate that you would say that."*

What happens next? Ninety-five times out of a hundred, if Alan says that and stops talking, Bill will ask a neutral question—like, "Really, why not?" Suddenly, the playing field is level!

Alan can now say, "Well, frankly, our conversation was going so well, I really expected a different outcome. Can you help me out? Should I have done something differently here?"

The beauty of this approach is that, despite your admission of being surprised, you are actually confirming the principle that all responses are anticipated. In fact, *you have just positively influenced what will happen next in the relationship!* By saying, "I didn't anticipate that," you'll usually get much better information about exactly where you stand with the prospect. And that's what you want: the right information.

For instance, in this scenario, Bill might say, "Well, the truth is, Alan, we have to deal with an urgent project right now, and I can't even think about making any major telecom decision this quarter." Alan might reply, "Okay—when do you think you will be ready to continue our discussion?" Bill might set an appointment for the following month, instead of the following week—and the relationship would be moving forward. All because he said, *"I really didn't anticipate that you would say that!"*

Using this skill is part of a larger process I call "getting righted." It's one of the most important (and most frequently overlooked) steps in selling. If I say, "I didn't anticipate that you would say that," what I'm really saying is, "Help me out—I must have missed something. Tell me where I went wrong." In fact, I can use exactly those kinds of words to ask overtly for guidance from the prospect. I can also take advantage of the prospect's natural instinct to correct me by stating something I suspect *isn't* true and watching carefully for the reaction I get. ("Now, it sounds to me like your timing priorities might be to get this project in place by this spring." "Oh, no, we're trying to get moving much more quickly than that—by December fifteenth at the very latest.")

Recently, I was training a large group of sales representatives who worked in the communications industry. During the question-and-answer session, one of them said to me, "We never seem to get the information we need from the people we visit. They find direct questions intrusive. What's the best way to get someone to open up to you?"

I told him, "Make a mistake."

He stared at me for a moment, as though I were mad to suggest such a thing. Then I explained what I meant.

"If you build a mistake into your question," I said, "the other person's instinct will automatically be to correct you. By allowing yourself to be righted, you will get the right information, and the other person will be in a position of strength. The conversation will flow naturally, because you've allowed the other person to be correct."

As it happens, this is a strategy we teach all of our own salespeople. If we're interested in learning the name of a prospect's most important competitor, we won't just ask, "Who's your most important competitor?" Instead, we'll say something like this: "I'm just curious—who do you consider to be your most significant competition. Would it be Flapjack Industries?" (This is assuming that we have a good idea that Flapjack Industries is *not* the company's most important competitor.)

The prospect instantly offers a correction: "Oh, no, it's not Flapjack—they're much too small for us to worry about. We're up against a much bigger outfit. Our main competition is ABC Industries."

Can you see how it works? Within just a few seconds, we've built rapport, allowed the other person a position of dominance in the conversation, *and* uncovered an essential piece of information.

Not long ago, this "build in a mistake" strategy helped one of our reps secure a major series of training dates from a huge electronics firm that was preparing its people for a new product launch. By carefully incorporating a few *faulty* assumptions within the questioning sequence, we were able to get information that had not been released to our competitors—information we used to develop a customized proposal that landed an account worth several hundred thousand dollars. To win that sale, we had to put aside the salesperson's typical concern for "being right" and find a way to get corrected!

With a few thoughtfully constructed questions and a little practice, you can take advantage of this powerful questioning strategy. Try it!

Don't worry about being "right"—get *righted*. The idea of including a conscious mistake while interviewing a client may seem unorthodox, but doing so can point you toward information you won't get in any other way.

THE BOTTOM LINE: "Getting righted" (by saying something like "I didn't anticipate you'd say that," or "Help me figure out where I went wrong," or "It seems to me that such-and-such is a priority for you") can be an extremely effective information-gathering strategy. Use it to get the prospect to react, and you will be more likely to determine what is really going on in the relationship—and how it should move forward.

Beware
"Casual Friday"

"I'm visiting a prospect next Friday who has informed me that once a week, team members at his organization 'dress down' for casual day. This Friday is such a day. In order to fit in, should I yield to my instinct to wear jeans and a turtleneck when I go in for my appointment?"

––––––––––––––

No!

This is a question on which we've had a good deal of first-hand experience at my company. The evidence is overwhelming: You cannot win—and can only lose—if you opt to "go casual" during a visit to a prospect's facility. No matter what the prospect says, no matter what the weather outside your window looks like, no matter how comfortable you feel with your contact, your best option is *always* to dress professionally for sales appointments.

The same principle, of course, applies to companies you visit where "casual day" extends into "casual week"—in other words, workplaces where *everyone*, from the head of the company on down, makes a habit of showing up for work each and every day in chinos, T-shirts, or similarly "relaxed" attire. Even when visiting such a workplace, dressing to "match" the laid-back fashion standards of your prospects is a big mistake.

Why? Consider these points.

• First and foremost, by dressing casually, you send the wrong message about your role. As a salesperson, you are going up against the status quo—that which the company is already doing. Never forget: You are a messenger of professional change. That means your recommendations must not be mistaken for those of an employee, and they should certainly not be mistaken for those of a mere social acquaintance. Think consultant—not beach buddy. After all, which one would you trust with the future of *your* business?

- Second, by dressing casually, you send the message that *nothing special is happening*. Something special *is* happening. You've shown up!
- Third, by dressing casually, you reduce your negotiating leverage. When you're finalizing a fee structure or winning a critical date on the calendar, aren't you more comfortable bringing all the authority and impact you can possibly muster to the discussion?
- Fourth, by dressing casually, you send the wrong message to your own employer—and to anyone of importance who may stroll through your facilities while you're dressed to underwhelm. ("Why on earth is he dressed like that today?") Perhaps the laid-back company wants to *hire* you because of the great job you did. Great! That still doesn't mean you should dress like Oscar Madison on the sales call. The only time you should ever dress casually is when you spend the *entire* day in your own office—and everyone else is doing the same.
- Finally, notice that, by dressing casually, you reduce your options for the rest of the day. Even if you haven't put off the

prospect at Company A by dressing like a shlub (and how certain can you ever be about that?), what about the prospect at Company B? When you limit your opportunities, you limit your earning power!

Sure, regional standards for appropriate business attire will vary. Sure, you'll dress differently when networking at a cocktail party than when networking at a trade show. Regardless, *dressing down costs you money.*

Taking the time and care to dress well for a meeting is universally understood business shorthand for "You should take what I'm saying seriously." Send that message!

Some salespeople say that dressing down makes them feel more "comfortable" because it constitutes "following the prospect's lead." (A side note: These are often the *same* salespeople who *don't* follow the prospect's lead when they're invited to coffee or lunch by a prospect; they're afraid they'll do something wrong, and they miss out on a chance to deepen the relationship.)

Let me close this chapter with a personal observation. All dressing down does for me is to remind me that I'm not earning what I could be. I don't know about you, but I'm not really comfortable with that! That's why we have a strict "dress-for-business" role at my company for sales reps preparing to go out on appointments—and we always will.

THE BOTTOM LINE: Never "go casual" during a meeting with a prospect.

Ask Key Questions about Your Best Accounts

"How do I increase the average value per account within my base of customers?"

———————

Recently, a client of ours in the telecommunications industry asked us to help set up a customized training program to help sales representatives increase sales depth within its base of existing customers. This client had numerous *Fortune* 100 customers—but had not developed a systemized way of identifying new areas for growth within each of these major accounts.

KEY QUESTIONS ABOUT THE TOP FIVE ACCOUNTS

We asked participants to bring information on their top five accounts to our training session. At the program, we asked them to answer the following questions about each account:

- How can I work with this company's sales department to win new customers—and increase profitability? *Follow-up:* What new people within the organization would I talk to about new customer development?
- How can I help the target company's sales, customer service, shipping, and transportation departments to maintain its base of existing accounts more effectively? *Follow-up:* What new people within the organization would I talk to about maintaining existing accounts?
- How can I work with the target company's shipping, accounts receivable, accounts payable, and manufacturing departments to improve communications with major suppliers? *Follow-up:* What new people within the organization would I talk to about improving

communications with suppliers?

- What programs can I put together with this company's marketing and sales departments to help the organization gain a competitive edge in the marketplace? *Follow-up:* What new people within the organization would I talk to about improving the company's competitive position?

- How can I help this company's department heads and human resources people retain and recruit high-quality employees? *Follow up:* What new people within the organization would I talk to about human resource issues?

- What can I propose to this company's shipping, receiving, dispatching, sales, and customer service people to help streamline transportation? *Follow-up:* What new people within the organization would I talk to about streamlining transportation activities?

In answering these questions, trainees were asked to identify contacts in at least five different areas within each company. They wrote down the size of each account, the possible product application by division/department, and information in each relevant area gleaned from sources like the Internet or the company's annual report.

At the end of this process, all the participants had a huge number of new prospects! Their new calling list was prioritized according to three criteria: territory management considerations (i.e., which contacts to meet with in the same building on a given day), the potential account size, and the likely time cycle. We then showed these reps how to build their calls around the groups and people they had helped in the past, thus dramatically increasing their likelihood of scheduling a meeting with the new person.

THE BOTTOM LINE: By asking these questions, you will be able to target and win new business within your major accounts—and beat quota.

Find Out What's Changed

"My work often involves customer service. What kinds of questions should I be asking to improve relationships with my company's clients?"

———————

Some months ago, I wandered into a Brooks Brothers store. My aim was simple: I wanted to buy a pair of suspenders. That was *all* I wanted to buy. The gentleman at the counter stared at me blankly when I stepped up and looked at him. Apparently, I thought to myself, I'm supposed to speak first. So I said, "I'm here to buy some suspenders." He pointed and said, "Over there."

Having received my marching orders, I

walked in the direction he had pointed. I picked out a single pair of suspenders. I paid for them. I left the store. That was the end of the exchange.

A week or so later, I went to an electronics store. Once again, my aim was simple: I wanted to buy a basic clock radio. (You know the kind: They run about $20.) A clock radio was *all* I wanted to buy. I meandered into the store. I stepped over to the counter and looked at the woman by the cash register. Although I was ready to speak first (my experience with the Brooks Brothers attendant had taught me something), I found to my surprise that, this time, I wasn't going to have to.

"Hi, there," the woman behind the counter said, smiling.

"Hi," I replied. "Can you show me where to find a $20 clock radio?"

Please bear in mind that that really was *all* I wanted to buy. And yet, at that point in the conversation, something amazing happened. The woman behind the counter said, "Sure. Just out of curiosity, though . . . what brings you to the store today?"

What a great question! She was actually interested in what had recently *changed* in my life. Clearly, *something* had changed enough to make me decide to walk into her store. She wasn't clear on precisely what it was, and she wanted to find out. So she asked. (After all, the odds were against my walking into the store on a Monday morning because I had nothing better to do, right?)

I answered her (refreshingly conversational) question by explaining that I had just moved to an apartment nearby, and that, since the apartment was bare, I had no way of waking up on time in the morning.

She smiled and showed me where the clock radios were. I picked out a model. Then she asked me whether I wanted to look at a television set. Well, that certainly made sense. I was camping out in an empty apartment; I was likely to be in California for a while, which meant I was in the market for a television; I'd already made the trip down to the electronics store. Why not at least take a look at a floor model or two? "Sure," I said. "Why don't you show me where those are and let me take a look at what you have." There were other questions as well. Did I want to look at CD players? Microwave ovens? Cordless telephones?

An hour after having walked into a store intending *only* to buy a $20 clock radio, I left with $2,000 in merchandise. All because one person had the sense to ask me about what I had *done* that had caused me to change my pattern and walk into her store.

Do *you* know what has recently changed in your prospect's or customer's life? When somebody calls you "out of the blue," do you ask some variation on "Just out of curiosity—what made you decide to call us today?"

THE BOTTOM LINE: Ask prospects "do-based" questions that focus on what has changed in their world. Do-based questions focus on what the other person is trying to accomplish, is doing right now, or has done in the past. For instance, "I'm just curious. What made you decide to get in touch with us?" That's a great strategy for salespeople—and anyone who interacts with customers and prospects.

Use E-mail Intelligently

"I'm a manager. What strategies and standards regarding e-mail messages should I share with my sales team?"

———————

Here are ten proven strategies for using e-mail persuasively with prospects and customers.

1. *Use a spell-check program.* Read every e-mail message at least two times before you send it. For particularly important messages, compose your message in a word processor and print out a copy. Ask a colleague to check your style and spelling before you send the message.

2. *Review both the topic and the content of your message closely before you send it.* Ask yourself whether your e-mail message is appropriate for all the individuals to whom it could be forwarded in a given organization. Remember that it is easy for your recipient to send your message to dozens or hundreds of people. If you're passing along performance assessments, remarks about company politics, or "frank" opinions about the people in your world or your prospect's world, think twice before you transmit those sensitive messages via e-mail.

3. *Never use all lowercase or all capital letters in an e-mail message.* Find other ways to impart a relaxed tone or to add emphasis to your writing. Adopting an informal tone is fine . . . varying from the rules of standard written English, while sometimes appropriate, will generally detract from the overall level of professionalism of your message.

4. *Archive messages you need for your records; delete the rest.* Good file maintenance eliminates confusion and

reduces the chances of mistakenly forwarding a message to the wrong person.

5. *Include a clear, concise, and inviting headline in the subject line.* The best kind of headline builds interest by helping the reader identify both the topic of your message and its relevance. (For example: "Directions to next week's sales training program.")

6. *Include your name and contact information when sending or responding to e-mail.* Your e-mail management software includes a feature that allows you to compose a consistent electronic "signature" that appears automatically at the end of each message. Use this feature as "virtual stationery" that identifies you, establishes your position within your organization, and passes along your contact information.

7. *Check your own e-mail daily.* In today's business environment, this is just as important as checking your phone messages!

8. *When writing for distribution to a large group, protect the privacy of your recipients' addresses by entering them on the "BCC:" line, rather than the "CC:" line.* "BCC" stands for "blind

carbon copy." Addresses entered on this line do not appear within the message. (If you wish to specify who is receiving a message without disclosing everyone's e-mail address, you can include the full names of your intended recipients at the beginning of your message.)

9. *Avoid sending hasty responses to inquiries you receive via e-mail.* A curt, one-sentence response to a customer, contact, or colleague is easier to send than most people imagine; such a message may be misinterpreted. If you don't have time to respond in full to a question or problem, say so in your e-mail message and follow up appropriately later.

10. *Think twice.* Never send an e-mail message composed in anger.

THE BOTTOM LINE: Follow the ten commandments of e-mail etiquette.

When in Doubt, Ask for the Appointment

"How can I get more face-to-face
meeting with prospects?"

Ask for them!

I make appointments with any and every
salesperson who calls me to ask for a face-to-
face meeting. I don't screen my calls. I don't
make salespeople jump through hoops. If they
want to meet with me, I try to meet with
them.

This is a rule I've developed over the
years. I make a point of living up to it—as
long as the travel demands of my training
schedule don't make it impossible for me to
do so. The ground rules are very simple: If
I'm going to be in my New York office, and
you call me up and ask me for a meeting, I'll

schedule a slot for you. It may be an *early* appointment, and it may not be for that week, but you will get a commitment for a face-to-face appointment.

I take this approach because I like to see and hear what real, live salespeople are doing. If they've come across a strategy that works on the phone or in person, I want to know about it. By the same token, if they're doing something that *doesn't* work, I want to know about that, too.

Here's the million-dollar question. If all any salesperson has to do to get a meeting with me is call me up . . . why, then, do I end up scheduling so few meetings with salespeople?

Take last week. I had hardly any travel commitments, and I spent almost the entire week in my New York City office. And yet I didn't sit down with a single outside salesperson.

That wasn't because I hadn't received calls from salespeople over the previous weeks. I had! Sometimes I get half a dozen of those calls in a single day. The problem is that I only schedule appointments with people who come out and *ask* me for a meeting—and *hardly anyone ever asks me directly for an appointment!*

Instead, they hem and haw and ask all kinds of "probing questions" that distract them from the purpose of their call. That purpose, presumably, is to set an appointment with me so the two of us can sit down and talk about whether it would make sense for me to use their product or service. Somehow this topic hardly ever comes up.

It's become something of a running joke around our office. I always put the calls on speakerphone so people can hear how callers will do everything *except* ask for a meeting. Everyone on my staff knows that all the salesperson has to do is suggest a date and time— I'll say "Yes." But for some reason the salespeople I speak to have a very hard time actually suggesting an appointment.

Here's an actual recent example of such a phone call. Someone calls me up and asks, "Are you currently investing in the stock market?"

I say, "Yes."

He says, "Are you using a broker right now?"

I say, "Yes."

He says, "Are you investing in such and such an area?"

I say, "Yes."

He says, "Would you mind if I sent you some materials about our company?"

I say, "No, I wouldn't mind that."

At that point, he says "Thank you" and tells me he hopes we can meet face to face very soon. Then he hangs up!

If he'd simply asked me, "Can we set up a meeting?" my answer would have been "Yes!"

How many other relationships could these salespeople move forward by focusing a little less on those "probing questions"? How many people might they meet if they actually made a direct *request* for a meeting during a cold call?

THE BOTTOM LINE: Don't get distracted by so-called "probing questions" at the opening stage of the relationship. Ask directly for an appointment when you make prospecting calls.

Don't Try to Close

"What's the best closing technique?"

_____

The best closing technique is (drum roll) . . . not having one!

People talk a lot about "closing" in sales. Our real objective, though, should not be to "close a sale" based on what we imagine the other person needs, but to get people to *use* our service (forever!) because doing so makes sense to *them*.

After all, people don't buy because of what we think they "need"—they buy because it makes sense to them to do so, based on what they're trying to accomplish. After all, if they "needed" our product or service so badly, they would have gone out and gotten it before we bothered to contact them!

STOP GUESSING

So, how do we come up with a plan that makes sense? Many sales reps simply guess. They cover their eyes and hope they will come up with something that matches what the prospect is actually doing. Sometimes what they propose matches. Most of the time it doesn't.

A typical high-pressure "close" tries to manipulate the other person into buying—by, for instance, building up the person's ego, making "concessions" that aren't really concessions at all, or even misrepresenting the facts surrounding the sale, the company, or the product or service. Anyone who's ever seen the movie *Glengarry Glen Ross* will remember the sequence in which Al Pacino tries to retain the money of a customer who wants a refund by pretending to close *another* sale with a high-powered senior executive who happens to be in the office at the time. (This is supposed to impress the fellow who wants the refund.) Actually, the high-powered senior executive, played by Jack Lemmon, is Pacino's colleague and fellow salesperson; the two are concocting an elaborate charade for the benefit, if that's the word, of their wary customer.

Talk about a "closing trick"! It's a tribute

to the realism of the script that this under-handed and manipulative effort to retain a customer with cold feet ultimately fails.

Though outright fraud is (thankfully) somewhat less common in the real world of selling than on the back lots of Hollywood, similarly shady "closing tricks" are still very much in evidence. A number of books outlining such stunts have been extremely successful.

Let's leave dishonest closing maneuvers out of the picture entirely, because they have less to do with selling than they do with swindling. The question I'd like to put on the table is, can someone *eventually* sell *something* using manipulative or high-pressure closing techniques (like the old classic, "Here's a pen—press hard when you sign the contract, you're making three copies")?

Sure. In fact, our experience is that you will sell one-third of all the prospects you meet with—no matter what you do—simply because you go out and see enough people. In other words, a good many salespeople sell without gathering a great deal of meaningful information, simply because they show up at the right time. The fancy "closing strategy" they use is more or less meaningless.

By the same token, one-third of the customers who could come your way will decide *not* to work with you, no matter what you do. You lose these accounts simply because the competition is there ahead of you or because of other problems you can't overcome.

When we step back and look at those two potential segments of our customer base, we realize that one-third is still up for grabs. That's the third we have to concentrate on. That's the third in which our actions can affect the outcome.

START MAKING SENSE

The aim is to develop a plan that will make sense to the other person, because we want to win as many of those "top third" sales as we possibly can. But we can't build that plan unless we *understand* what they're trying to do!

To do that, we have to get information about the prospect by asking questions, which I'll discuss in Chapters 6, 17, 18, and 21 in this book.

As you'll learn a little later on, there are four steps to the ideal selling process:

1. Opening (qualifying)
2. Information gathering (interviewing)
3. Presentation (sharing the plan based on what we've learned makes sense to the other person)

4. Closing (reaching the point at which the other person agrees to use our product or service)

The second step—the interview step—is the make-or-break part of the relationship. That's where we gather information that allows us to put together the right plan. Everything else in the relationship hinges on the questions we ask at that point.

THE BOTTOM LINE: Don't imagine you know what the other person "needs." Instead, focus your attention on gathering facts so you can build a plan that makes sense based on what he or she is doing.

Raise Tough Issues Yourself

"Help! I have no idea what's really
happening in the target company.
How do I find out?"

One of the biggest challenges salespeople face is learning where a prospect stands on a given issue.

If you go into a meeting and have a "gut feeling" that a prospect has doubts about some aspect of working with you, how do you confirm your instinct? Most salespeople hesitate to ask a person directly for an opinion; they initiate a long discussion about other topics instead of directly raising important questions. This approach is usually counterproductive, and always a waste of time.

Suppose you meet with a prospect and think that his or her biggest issue about using your products is resistance to your price. Here's the four-step strategy to use:

1. *Say* that you are unhappy or concerned.
2. *Wait* for the prospect to ask "Why?" (He or she *always* will.)
3. *Raise* the issue you're unsure about briefly.
4. *Listen* to the prospect's response.

For instance: On your next meeting, you might decide to walk into the prospect's office, sit down, and say, "I'm really concerned," and then *stop talking*. The decision-maker will reply, "Why?" Your answer: "Because I don't think my price is competitive."

You've raised the issue yourself. This type of statement will allow the prospect to respond honestly. Count on it: If you listen to the decision-maker, you will soon know *exactly* what he or she thinks about your pricing.

A client in the health care industry called me the other day. She was uncertain about the status of an upcoming enrollment with a major prospect. She and her prospect had tentatively discussed setting an enrollment meeting with the target company's employees for the following month, but there had been no action.

Was there a problem? Was the prospect planning to put off the enrollment indefinitely? If not, why had there been no action?

The question we faced was really a pretty simple one: Did the prospect have a timing obstacle, and, if so, what was it? On my advice, our client called her prospect and said, "I'm concerned about the enrollment for August that we discussed."

The prospect said, "Really? Why is that?"

"I'm afraid that we don't have enough time to get this meeting together for you," our client answered.

The prospect responded, "You know what? I'm concerned, too. Let's set the dates right now." Problem solved!

Take a good look at your current prospect base. Are you uncertain about a prospect's reaction to your pricing? Call that person right now and use the four-step process you've just learned to raise the pricing issue. Are you concerned about a person's level of comfort with a product's warranty? Use this strategy to raise the issue yourself; listen closely to what you hear in response. Are you unsure whether a prospect agrees with your assessment of a product's scalability? *Raise the issue yourself!*

Follow the four steps. I guarantee that you will get a reaction from the other person that lets you know immediately what you have to focus on.

Here's an alternative approach that uses basically the same principle. Sometimes I'll find myself walking a new prospect through a preliminary proposal, and I won't have any idea what the prospect thinks of my pricing. (Actually, this doesn't happen all *that* often, as I've picked up some skill over the years at reading people's body language, but it does happen from time to time.) When I have absolutely no idea what the person's reaction to my pricing is, and the relationship is a little too young for me to feel comfortable with the "I'm concerned" approach, I may say something else. I may say, "You know, this is the point where people typically have a problem with price if that's an issue for them." Then I *stop talking*.

What have I done? I've just given the person permission to talk about my pricing. Nine times out of ten, he or she will open up. The person's response to this simple statement *virtually always* tells me where I stand.

Remember, it is your job to uncover the

real issue at hand! Many prospects will say that they object to pricing, while they are really covering up some other concern. It is your responsibility to ask questions and determine what (if anything) is preventing you from working together.

THE BOTTOM LINE: Use this simple strategy to find out exactly where a prospect stands on any given issue. You don't have to initiate a long discussion. All you have to do is *raise the issue*. As you will learn quickly, the prospect or customer will do most of the talking!

Get More Return Phone Calls

"I can't seem to get people to return my calls. I leave messages, but nothing happens. Any suggestions?"

At least you're leaving messages. Most of the salespeople we run into don't! You should always leave a message for your contact when you're making prospecting calls. My bet is that if you leave the right kind of message, you're more likely to get a curious call back. That puts the contact in a better mindset to consider meeting with you.

Here are two strategies to implement that will improve your return-call results immediately.

75 PERCENT RETURN CALLS

The following message format has resulted in 75 percent return calls. Use it!

"Hi, it's Bob Black—my number is 212-555-1212, and I'm calling from ABC Company. This is regarding the Huge Customer of Ours in Your Industry. I look forward to speaking with you soon."

This assumes, of course, that the company you reference is one of your satisfied customers. When the person calls back, you *must* use the work you've done with the company you mentioned as your reason for the call.

99 PERCENT RETURN CALLS

If you are calling someone who has been called by a rep in your company, use that person as the reference in your message.

"Hi, it's Bob Black. I'm calling you about our representative, Jane Myers, who spoke to you last month. Please call me at 212-555-1212."

This technique has resulted in 99 percent return calls! When you get the call back, you can simply say, "My records show that Jane spoke with you last month about working with us—and I wanted to find out where things went wrong." You will find that two very interesting things happen when you do this. First, the contact will become extremely protective of the person he or she met with. Second, the person you're calling will almost always reveal exactly what is standing in the way of your working together—even if he or she avoided discussing this with your colleague in the past. The person's explanation will usually begin with the words, "The thing is . . ."

When you start using the message strategies I've outlined in this chapter, you will want to make a habit of keeping easy-to-retrieve notes on who you're calling and why. If you get taken by surprise by a return call (and it's a pretty good bet that you will), you can retain momentum in the conversation by saying:

"Ms. Jones, thank you so much for returning my call—let me get my notes for you. Would you mind holding on for just a moment?"

This is an honest, direct, and completely professional request that will win you the few seconds you need to grab your file, notebook, or Palm Pilot and retrieve the information you need to reorient yourself.

THE BOTTOM LINE: Use these two simple strategies to dramatically increase the number of return calls you get when you leave messages.

Don't Bring Everything!

"I don't know what to say at the end of the appointment. The prospect tells me we've covered everything in detail and that he/she needs to talk to other people about what my organization offers. I can't seem to get a next step. What do I do?"

———————

There are a number of reasons meetings with promising prospects don't result in a next step. However, one of the most common problems in this area—having no reason to come back—is also one of the easiest to fix.

Think about it. When we've "covered everything" with the prospect, we appear to have left ourselves no reason to come back for that all-important second meeting! Solution: Don't cover everything during the first meeting with the prospect!

Specifically, *don't bring everything*. Bring *enough* in the way of testimonials, references, articles, books, and similar sales tools to give your meeting a purpose and a sense of structure. But leave something for the second meeting, so you can say something like this as the meeting draws to a close:

"You know what? You really ought to take a look at what we've been doing in the area of customized training for people in the widget industry. I should bring you some of the materials we've put together on that. Why don't I come by again next Tuesday at two o'clock and show you one of the projects we've been working on?"

If you bring the essentials—and *only* the essentials—to your initial meeting with a prospect, you'll have a built-in "reason to come back." If you make the most of it, you'll run into fewer prospects who will tell you that they've heard everything they need to hear during the first meeting.

(For more on conducting a great first meeting with a prospect, see Skills 14–17.)

THE BOTTOM LINE: Resist the temptation to bring everything to the first meeting; leave yourself a reason to come back for the second one.

Don't "Product Dump"

"I give what I think is a great opening summary of my company and its products and services during the opening phase of the first meeting. It takes fifteen to twenty minutes. Prospects don't seem to be responding well to it, though. What's happening?"

What's happening is you're forgetting one of the most important facts of professional sales: *You are more than a walking brochure!*

Most salespeople are taught to "find the needs" of their prospects, so they can make presentations designed to show how their organizations can fill those "needs." In fact, they get used to six or eight common "needs" and become very comfortable indeed discussing them.

There's a problem with this approach, though. It turns you into a walking advertisement. You recite a familiar "spiel" during your first meeting. Guess what? In today's economy, the odds are high that your prospect already has—or has access to—some variation on what you offer. He or she doesn't really "need" you at all.

The act of reciting a well-known (and lengthy) monologue to a prospect is called "throwing up" on the prospect—or, to use a slightly more pleasant term, executing a "product dump." Whatever we call it, it means we are sending far more information *out* during the first meeting than we are taking *in*. In fact, product dumping is the most common reason for a first meeting with a prospect *not* to go well. Prospects hate hearing a product dump during the first meeting. (Don't you?)

How to Turn Prospects Off

Reciting what we think we know about familiar "needs" during initial meetings with prospects won't help us to sell more efficiently. In assessing people's needs, we usually assume we know all about their business already. We assume that this prospect is facing exactly the same situation as the last prospect we met with. So we just soliloquize about what we have to offer or read from a brochure. In so doing, we overlook opportunities to gather meaningful information about what's actually going on in the life of the person we're talking to. The result: another turned-off prospect.

The reason so many salespeople rely on product dumps is that meetings with prospects can be stressful. When we're stressed, we fall back on what's familiar to us—namely, what we know about our product or service. Unfortunately, when we do that, we close down the lines of communication.

Not long ago, we had a visit from a salesperson who represented a copier company. The meeting consisted of a brief exchange of greetings, a couple over superficial remarks about the weather and the traffic, and the salesperson's spiel about the features of his machine. This spiel went on, uninterrupted, for twenty minutes, at the conclusion of which time the fellow tried to "close" me. He didn't succeed. He tried again. He didn't succeed. He packed up his things and left.

Why do I share this story with you? Because I want you to understand the real reason I didn't even consider buying from this young man. *He never asked me what business*

I was in.

Can you imagine? Here he is trying to sell me a $15,000 copier, and he has no idea what I plan to use it for!

Don't try to sell that way. Don't let your nervousness shut down the possibility of learning the most elementary facts about the person you're talking to. Don't miss out on a chance to find out a little bit more about your prospect than that stressed-out copier sales-person did.

In the next two chapters, you'll find strategies for conducting a great face-to-face discussion with your prospect.

THE BOTTOM LINE: Avoid product dumps. They turn prospects off.

Beyond "Slapshot" Selling

"I just had a meeting with a prospect that didn't go well. Point by point, I matched everything the competition offered, but I couldn't get the person to agree to another meeting with me. What should I have done differently?"

———

If you've ever had a first meeting with a prospect that appeared to meander, that didn't result in a next step—but should have—you're in good company. Just about every salesperson has had the experience of watching a potentially good meeting stray into "thanks but no thanks" territory. Often, we lose control of these meetings because we didn't structure them correctly—or, worse, didn't try to structure them at all!

Slapshot selling is argumentative, "kneejerk" selling that spends more time batting away objections than it does finding out about meaningful information that illuminates the prospect's objectives and activities. Slapshot selling is inflexible and geared toward regaining the opportunity to talk. Slapshot selling is selling that says, "Please keep your comments to yourself and let me finish my PowerPoint show." Slapshot selling is not a particularly efficient way to sell. It's also a poor way to begin a business relationship.

YOUR TRUE COMPETITION ISN'T WHO YOU THINK IT IS

Let's start our examination of how to structure the first meeting by examining an unspoken component of it: the competition we face.

In our training seminars, we make a habit of asking people who their most important competition is. The answers we get usually sound like this:

- "Our most important competition is Huge Well-Financed Company."
- Or: "Our most important competition is Little Innovative Company."

- Or: "Our most important competition is ourselves."

While all of these answers are interesting, none of them is correct. In fact, the most important competition you face is *what the prospect is already doing.*

You have to find out what your prospect is doing and how he or she could do it differently. You are a messenger of change—but you can't change what makes sense to the prospect if you don't know what that is!

Again—don't get distracted by what you think the person or organization "needs." Ask yourself: If your prospect actually needed to change that status quo, wouldn't he or she have taken action to do so already?

So: What the person is *doing right now* is your true competitor.

BEYOND "SLAPSHOT" SELLING

What have we learned so far in this chapter and in the previous one?

We know that finding out what *we* think the person needs probably isn't going to help us much. And we know that our true competition is what the person is already doing.

In fact, finding out what the person we're talking to has done in the past, is doing now, and wants to do in the future will give us the very best opportunity to discuss the ways we may be able to help the prospect meet key goals.

Our primary selling goal must be to find out what the person's trying to achieve now—and learn whether we can help him or her do that better. Learning what's on the list of "Important Things to Accomplish"—and whether we can help turn those objectives into realities—makes much more sense than attempting to impose some predetermined solution based solely on our own preconceptions.

What's the best way to find out what the person is doing? Ask do-based questions. Let's assume we're selling investment management services.

Here's a classic example of a question that focuses on what the person's actually doing right now—and illuminates the status quo:

"I'm just curious—What would you have done (to develop an investment portfolio/plan for retirement/save for college) if I hadn't called you?"

This kind of "do-based" questioning doesn't exist in a vacuum. It takes place within an overall sales process. The process has four steps—Opening, Interviewing, Presentation, and Closing—and the goal of any step is always to get to the next step and, ultimately, to step four. Look closely at the diagram below, which outlines the ideal sales cycle we discussed in Chapter 12.

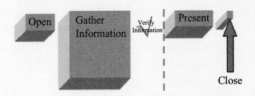

Of the four steps, which do you think should consume the majority of your time?

Please examine this diagram very closely indeed before you proceed any further in this book. Note that in the ideal sale, you should do roughly 75 percent of your work *before* the presentation.

Do you realize what that means? It means that if we've gathered the right information about what makes sense to the prospect *now*, our recommendation (or plan) about what should happen *next* will make sense, too. If it does, our close will be mercifully brief (and very easy).

So—how does all this affect your planning for the initial meeting? Well, during your first meeting, you will aim to move from the opening into the information-gathering step. You will *not* attempt to deliver a long monologue, and you certainly won't attempt to close the sale!

If we try to "always be closing," we'll be just as inefficient as everyone else. Instead of the model we just saw, our process will look like what most salespeople do, which is this:

There's a big opening—that's the product dump—then there are a few questions that focus on the "needs" the salesperson assumes exist. The salesperson might ask, "Are you getting X?" The prospect says, "No, we're getting Y." And the salesperson says, "Well, that's okay, because we offer Y, too." *Slapshot!* The product dump continues—even though the salesperson has no idea what made the prospect choose Y over X, how Y was selected, or whether Z is under consideration as a replacement.

Then there's a big attempt to make a presentation and an even bigger attempt to close. All without enough information!

AVOIDING "SLAPSHOT" SELLING IN THE FIRST MEETING

Individual investors, for instance, are often surprised, and a little annoyed, to be informed during the first meeting that they "need" more help with their investment portfolio. And yet that's what most of the people who try to sell them are actually saying: "We already know what you need; we already know what you're getting; we've got something better."

We can't assume we know what the other person's unique aspirations are if we don't ask about them during the first meeting! But *how* should we ask about those aspirations in a way that will keep the other person from freezing up on us? How, exactly, should we launch the information-gathering phase?

The answer lies in using a flexible questioning and interviewing model. We know that we want to find out what the prospect *does*. But the questions we pose to uncover that information can't simply be recited one after another. We have to let the prospect's responses affect the direction of the discussion. Otherwise, it's not a great sales meeting—it's an interrogation. News flash: Prospects don't like interrogations.

By contrast, in the best sales meetings, *we* get to pose "big" questions, and the *prospect* gets to set the agenda within the area covered by each of those "big" questions. Fortunately, there's a pattern—a roadmap—we can follow to make exactly this kind of discussion happen. We call it the PIPA Sequence. And we'll be examining it in depth in the next chapter. For now, remember this: Slapshot selling—the kind of selling that happens when nervous salespeople try to "take control" of the discussion by firing off memorized questions or reciting product information—is guaranteed to get prospects to tune out.

THE BOTTOM LINE: Don't engage in "slapshot" selling.

Master PIPA (Learn the Art of Conducting a Great First Meeting)

"I don't know how to handle the transition out of the 'small talk' phase of the meeting. What's the best strategy?"

The PIPA sequence can help you here. It looks like the chart on the following page.

This PIPA outline can produce spectacular results for you from the very first moments of your initial meeting with the prospect. Let's see how the sequence works at the beginning of a meeting. (Note: The PIPA sequence can be adapted to virtually any point in any conversation, but it's easiest to understand if you apply it to the beginning of any discussion.)

The PIPA Sequence: Roadmap for Great Conversations

As a matter of social convention, "ice-breaker" questions—questions that help you build rapport and a sense of commonality with the other person—are likely to begin your meeting. Bear in mind, though, that even these kinds of questions can be pointed in a direction that illuminates your prospect's unique situation. For instance:

"I'm just curious, how does someone get to be a (Vice President of Widget Reclamation/Senior Data Analyst/CEO/etc.)?"

Once you have completed this small talk portion of your initial meeting, you will be ready to make a seamless transition into the "business" segment of the meeting. The first

"P" in the PIPA sequence will help you do just that.

THE FIRST "P" IN PIPA

After the brief "get-acquainted" portion of the meeting draws to a close (usually indicated by a sizable pause), direct the meeting toward the business at hand by asking something along the following lines:

"Mr. Prospect, would it help if I told you a little bit about our company and what we do?"

By doing this, you are *presenting* an option—that is to say, implementing the first "P" in the PIPA sequence.

This question—which virtually always yields a yes answer—is *not* an excuse to execute a product dump.

In the unlikely event that the prospect tells you he or she *doesn't* want to hear about what you and your company do, but has something else pressing to discuss, simply follow the prospect's lead. The information-gathering phase of the meeting has begun with virtually no effort from you on the transition.

THE "I" IN PIPA—INTERVIEWING

The "would it help if I told you a little bit about us" question points us toward a *con-*

cise, bare-bones statement of our own experience and the company's history. It might sound like this:

> "Well, ABC Widget Development is the largest specialized widget manufacturing company in the United States. We've been in business since 1923, and I've been working for the company as a senior account representative since 1997."

We must now *immediately* pose a question that meets three qualifications:

1. It focuses on what the prospect does.
2. It focuses on some broadly defined area where we have added value for other customers.
3. It is likely to be easy for the prospect to answer.

The moment we pose this "do-focused" question in an area in which we feel we can add value, we are seamlessly making the transition into the second, and most important, part of the PIPA sequence—gathering *information*. So we would conclude our "little bit about us" statement by saying, "Mr.

Prospect, I'm just curious, have you ever worked with a custom widget manufacturer before?"

(A side note: "I'm just curious" and "By the way" are extremely effective phrases for introducing questions.)

Look at the critical transition out of small talk once again.

- Small talk (builds rapport, establishes commonality; may include illuminating questions about the person's past, such as, "How does someone become a . . . ?")
- We ask: "Would it help if I told you a little bit about us?" (The prospect will virtually always agree.)
- We deliver a brief commercial. (Two or three sentences should probably be your outer limit.)
- We immediately ask a question that focuses on what the prospect does, addresses an area where we have added value in the past to other customers, and is probably easy for the prospect to answer.

And here's what the transition might sound like in action. Note again that the question must be posed *immediately* after our brief commercial.

> "Well, ABC Widget Development is the largest specialized widget manufacturing company in the United States. We've been in business since 1923, and I've been working for the company as a senior account representative since 1997. I'm just curious, have you ever worked with a specialized widget manufacturer before?"

Strategize Your First Question

Know the first question you plan to ask after the small talk section concludes!

There is simply no excuse for "winging" the first question in the "I" portion of the PIPA sequence. Let's assume our company offers investment services. On the next page are examples of "do-based" questions that could be a good starting point for our discussion. Each could help you make the transition from "Would it help if I told you a little bit about us?" to gathering information.

- If prospect contacted you: I'm just curious—what made you decide to call *us* about investment strategies?

- If you contacted the prospect: I'm just curious—what were you going to do if I hadn't gotten in touch with you?
- I'm just curious—have you ever worked with an investment advisor before?
- Really? How did you choose them?
- I'm just curious—what kinds of investments have you focused on in the past?
- How did they work out for you?

Where Do You Go from There?

Broadly speaking, you want to explore the *past*, the *present*, and the *future*—with "big" questions that focus on *how* or *why*. For instance:

- Past: "What results did you expect from that approach?" Possible follow-up: "How did you decide whether or not to continue doing that?"
- Present: "What are you doing now in this area?" Possible follow-up: "Why did you choose to work with XYZ company?"
- Future: "What would you personally like to accomplish in this area?" Possible follow-up: "How will you measure whether or not you're getting closer to that goal?"

Make Sure You Know the Basics

Even though you should *never* try to impose a predetermined sequence of questions on your prospect, there are certain essential pieces of information you should always try to secure at some point during the first meeting.

Specifically, you should not consider the first meeting a success unless you have recorded, in written form, the following:

- The essentials of the prospect's work history
- The kinds of internal and external customers the prospect must keep happy on a regular basis
- What the prospect is trying to accomplish
- The standards used for previous purchase decisions in your area

A great way to learn the decision-making process in past purchase decisions is to ask, "Why did you decide to do it that way?" or "How did you choose them?"

THE SECOND "P" IN PIPA—PRESENT A NEXT STEP OPTION

Once you have gathered enough information to get a sense of where the relationship should go next, you'll be in a great position to use the second "P" in PIPA. You will present a next step recommendation.

It could sound like this:

"Based on what you've told me today—specifically X, Y, and Z—I think I should put together a preliminary proposal to give you an idea of what we might be able to do for you in this area. Why don't I come back here next Tuesday at two o'clock?"

Always ask for a next step that's easy, logical, and helpful and that's connected to a specific date and time. Make the subject of your conversation *when* you'll be meeting next, not *whether* you'll be meeting next. See what happens!

By the way, the second "P" in PIPA also reminds you of *"parable selling"*—which is an excellent way to use your organization's success stories to *position* yourself for the next step. This is often (but not always!) a preliminary to presenting a next step option.

Parable selling sounds like this: "It's interesting that you mention XYZ challenge—that's very similar to the situation I faced with my last customer, Tommy Bigshott. What we found was . . . " You might conclude with: "Why don't I come back here next Tuesday at two o'clock and show you the plan I put together for Bigshott?"

THE "A" IN PIPA—AGREEMENT THAT YOUR NEXT STEP MAKES SENSE

It's not enough simply to present a next step option. In the "A" portion of the PIPA sequence, you make sure that the other person specifically *agrees* to the step you have proposed.

Your prospect may agree immediately with the next step you suggest. Then again, he or she may offer a confusing or uncertain response. When this happens, you will want to tactfully but firmly move the issue to the forefront by exploring whether or not what you've suggested *makes sense*.

The best way to find out about this is simply to ask: "So—do you think it makes sense for us to get together again at this time next week?"

The beauty of this approach is that if it *doesn't* make sense to the other person, he or she will usually explain *why* it doesn't!

If the person doesn't provide any information about why the next step you've proposed doesn't make sense, use the "I didn't anticipate that" technique outlined below.

You: So—do you think it makes sense for us to get together again next Tuesday at two o'clock?

Prospect: I'd really rather not.

You: I'll be honest—that's a surprise to me. I didn't anticipate that you'd say that. Usually, at this stage of the meeting, when we find out about X, Y, and Z, people are eager to learn what happens next, and they want to set up a time to do that. Did I do something wrong?

Prospect: Oh, no—it's nothing you did. The problem's on our end. You see, the thing is . . .

Those are the magic words: "The thing is . . ." Now you're going to hear more critical information. Be sure to take careful note of anything and everything that follows the words "The thing is"! This information is likely to be extremely important. (*Note:* You can learn more about the "I didn't anticipate that" approach in Chapter 4.)

THE BOTTOM LINE: Use the PIPA outline. If something goes wrong in the affirmation or agreement step, take responsibility! Be willing to ask, "Did I do something wrong?" Listen carefully for the magic words likely to come your way in response: "The thing is . . . "

Get Prospects to Open Up to You

"I can't seem to get prospects to open up to me during face-to-face meetings. Is there a simple way to encourage them to start talking during the information-gathering phase?"

———————

Yes. Pull out a yellow legal pad and a pen, pose a question, and then look away from your prospect—and look thoughtfully at the pad. Wait to see what happens.

What you will almost invariably find is that the simple act of writing down the date and company name will cause the person to open up to you. The same basic strategy applies if you're selling over the phone. Say something like, "Hold on a minute, I want to write that down," or "Just a second, let me pull out my pad so I can get this all down." Letting the prospect know that you are preparing to take notes, and riding out the small silence that may follow, virtually always leads to detailed answers to your questions.

Again—you can't make things happen in the sales relationship if you don't know what the prospect is trying to accomplish. And you usually can't find *that* out unless the prospect receives nonthreatening "talk to me" messages from you during the meeting. My experience is that the very best way to send those messages is by pulling out a pad and taking notes.

SENDING THE MESSAGE

Here are five great "talk to me" messages you send when you take notes during in-person meetings with prospects:

1. *"You are in control of this conversation."* (You're offering a good question now and again, but the prospect's response is what's driving the discussion.)
2. *"I am focused like a laser beam on finding out what you do."* (As opposed to being totally focused on, say, figuring out how to operate a PowerPoint

demonstration.)

3. *"I am organized."* (How many of the people your prospect runs into during the course of the average day go to the trouble of recording important instructions in permanent, hard-copy format?)

4. *"I am trustworthy."* (Tactful, engaged note taking has a remarkable way of encouraging prospects to elevate you to informal "insider" status.)

5. *"I consider you a 'bigshot.'"* (Hey—this person will determine whether or not you get a commission. If that doesn't equal "bigshot," nothing does.)

There's another advantage to taking notes, of course: When you do so, you can use your pad as a tool for sketching out your own diagrams and ideas relevant to your prospect's situation.

THE BOTTOM LINE: Always—repeat, always—take notes during discussions with clients.

Prepare Questions ahead of Time!

"I don't know what to ask during meetings with prospects. I always seem to fall back on talking about me, my company, or my product. What kinds of questions should I be asking?"

Here are a number of questions you should consider asking during the all-important information-gathering phase of your meeting. (If memorizing them is difficult, consider writing these—or others—down on your legal pad before you leave for the meeting!)

- "How's business?"
- "What would you have done in such-and-such an area if I hadn't called you?" (Or: "What made you decide to

call us?")

- "I'm just curious—what are you try-ing to make happen here over the next thirty days?"
- "I'm just curious—what do you do here?"
- "How does your company sell its product/service?"
- "How many people work here? Do they report to you?"
- "How many people do you work with who operate out of other locations?"
- "How do you maintain a competitive edge in an industry like this?"
- "How is your organization struc-tured? How many offices/locations do you have?"
- "What are you doing now to grow your business?"
- "What are you doing now to reach out to new customers?"
- "What are you doing now to stay close to your existing customers?"
- "What are you doing now to service your accounts better?"
- "What are you doing now to track what your branch offices are doing on a daily basis?"
- "What are you doing to make it

easier for customers to respond to your mailings?"
- "What made you decide to make X a priority right now?"
- "What kinds of new customers are you trying to attract?"
- "Who do you consider to be your biggest competitor? Why?"
- "How do you distinguish yourself from companies like X, Y, and Z in an industry like this?"
- "Is your industry changing? How?"
- "What was the last quarter/year like for you?"
- "Why did you decide to work with ABC Company?"

Whatever questions you ask, you should make a point of *reviewing them ahead of time*. As I've noted earlier, we tend to fall back on what is most familiar to us. Be sure that what's most familiar to *you* as you walk in the door to the meeting is the PIPA sequence and the first four or five questions (at least) that you'd like to ask during the course of the meeting.

THE BOTTOM LINE: Know—and practice— the first few questions you plan to ask at the meeting. This is vitally important because you will be in an unfamiliar setting with an unfamiliar person during your initial meeting. That equals stress, and during stressful situations, you will naturally revert to that which is most familiar to you.

Skill #19

Don't Present Too Early

"My closing ratio stinks. Why?"

In all likelihood, the answer is a simple one: You are trying to close *before* you've gathered enough information to make an intelligent recommendation.

Always remember: About three-quarters of your time must be invested in the work that comes *before* the presentation!

Ask yourself: Am I sure I'm talking to the right person? (This is either the decision-maker or the person who can get the decision made for you.) If the answer is *no*, you are not ready to make a formal presentation.

Ask yourself: Am I sure this plan makes

sense, based on what I know this person is actually trying to *do*? If the answer is *no,* you are not ready to make a formal presentation.

Ask yourself: Have I discussed all the budget issues with my contact? Does the pricing make sense? Raise the issue yourself—don't wait for the prospect to do so. If the answer is *no,* you are not ready to make a formal presentation.

Ask yourself: Have I established a realistic timetable? If the implementation or delivery schedule is still theoretical, there's a problem! You are not ready to make a formal presentation.

Ask yourself: Does my contact *know* I expect to close this sale? If you have any doubt, say something like this: "I'm going to gather everything we've done into a formal proposal for our meeting next Tuesday, and at that point, I don't see any reason why we wouldn't be able to finalize this." See what happens! This is an especially important point. If the contact does not know that you plan to close the sale, then you are *definitely* not ready to make a formal presentation.

If you're tempted to skip one of the steps outlined in this chapter, consider one more question. What makes more sense—delivering five customized proposals to five prospects who are "playing ball" with you—or delivering twenty-five *uncustomized* proposals that have little or nothing to do with what people are trying to accomplish?

THE BOTTOM LINE: Most salespeople make presentations before they're ready to. Don't be one of them.

Verify Your Information

"How can I be sure the presentation
I make matches what the prospect
is actually doing?"

———————

You can't—unless you verify the information
you've gathered.

Take another look at the four steps of
the selling cycle from the chart on the following page.

That dotted line between the information-
gathering and presentation steps represents a
substep—the part of the sale where you *verify*
that the information you *think* you've gathered really is accurate and complete.

Verifying is a very important concept. You

must be willing to be corrected, both to elicit new facts and to verify that you're ready to make the presentation. Some salespeople don't try to verify because they're afraid of making a mistake in front of the prospect. Guess what? If you *never* get corrected by the people you reach out to, you're not asking the right questions!

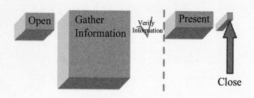

The best way to verify your information is by means of a preliminary proposal (also known as an outline). This short document is basically a two- or three-page summary that says, "I am not a proposal." It allows the prospect to give you feedback *before* you make a formal recommendation.

You want the person to write all over your outline and make all kinds of changes—so *you* know what kinds of changes to make (and terminology to adopt) before you make a formal recommendation. Once you've used your preliminary proposal to get "righted" during a meeting with the prospect, you can say, "Well, I think we've got everything in place. What I'd like to do is go back and make these changes and then come back here Friday at three o'clock. At that point, we should be able to finalize this and set your delivery dates. Does that make sense?"

When you say that, you'll know exactly where you stand. You'll know for sure whether you've verified the information properly.

THE BOTTOM LINE: Use a preliminary proposal, or outline, to verify your information.

Ask Yourself the Right Questions

"I'm nervous during my meetings with prospects. I'm new at selling with this company, and I feel like I still haven't mastered everything I should know about our company and its customers. Where should I start?"

In order to conduct an effective meeting with any prospect, you must be confident about the answers to three key questions about your own company.

QUESTION #1

Why do people buy from you? Complete the sentence: "People buy from us because . . ." Where, specifically, do you add value for your customers? Does your customer base include people who have chosen to work with you for a number of years? Why do they do that? Talk to your sales manager or to colleagues until you get a range of answers. Learn the relevant success stories.

QUESTION #2

What makes you different? Complete the sentence: "The main thing that distinguishes us from/makes us better than other companies that sell what we do is . . ." Again, work with your colleagues and superiors to develop relevant success stories. Be prepared for the prospect's (fair) question: "Why should I buy from you?"

QUESTION #3

What's more important than price to your customers? Complete the sentence: "Even though we might not be the least expensive option, people choose us because . . ." These are especially important success stories to learn—and repeat! If you are relying *solely* on price to win customers, you will not sell deeply or build loyalty in your customer base.

THE BOTTOM LINE: Your answers to each of these questions should lead you to stories or examples of success you or your organization has had with specific clients. Become familiar with those stories.

Know What You Want before You Even Walk in the Door

"My manager says I'm spending too much time researching the company and not enough time working out what should happen next in the relationship. Shouldn't I know *something* about the company before I go in?"

Don't over-research—but do spend a little time gathering the relevant facts. Find out the basics about the company. In today's selling environment, there is no excuse for "cluelessness" about the company's products and services. Take a few minutes to pull up the target company's Web site. Ask yourself: Who are this company's customers? Which of our success stories would be most relevant to this company?

When you've got the answers to these questions, you should probably move out of "research mode" and think about a different kind of preparation for the meeting.

It's just as important to know what kind of next step you plan to ask for at the conclusion of the meeting. In other words, what is the outcome you want from this meeting? Specifically: What are you planning to ask for at the conclusion of the meeting? Another meeting to review a preliminary proposal? Another meeting to connect with the president of the company? A phone conference at a specific date and time to review technical details? A formal commitment to work together?

Remember, the next step you ask for must be helpful, logical, and easy for the prospect to agree to. It must also be connected to a specific date and time. And you must ask for it *directly* before you leave the meeting.

Be sure you plan a *primary* next step—and a *backup* next step, just in case the first one doesn't work out.

THE BOTTOM LINE: Don't over-research, but do spend a little time gathering the relevant facts, perhaps via the Internet. Know what next step you plan to ask for—and prepare a backup, just in case the first one doesn't work out.

SKILL #23

Work Your Way up the Ladder

"Help! I'm stuck with a 'contact' who knows nothing about the service I'm selling. How do I hook up with the real decision-maker?"

———————————

If you *know for certain* that your contact cannot make the decision or get the decision made for you, tactfully ask a technical or logistical question your prospect will not be able to answer, but the true decision-maker *would* be able to answer.

When the person responds, "I don't know," you can say something like this: "Gee, that's actually pretty important. Who would we talk to about that?"

This is an excellent way to move "up the ladder" with your contact.

———————————

Your question could sound like this: "How long does the consumer usually have to wait for delivery once the order has been entered into the computer system?"

It's important to verify that the person you're talking to really is the decision-maker. When in doubt, ask a "how" or "why" question, like "Why did you choose that vendor?" or "How did you decide to do that?" These questions will point you toward the real decision-maker.

Ask detailed questions—and try to work with your contact to build alliances that will help you connect with the people who can get them answered.

Don't get misled by titles or organizational charts. Titles can be extremely misleading. A person can have the most impressive title in the world, but have literally no knowledge about the area of activity that title suggests. For instance, a media relations officer may have little or no talent for dealing with editors working under tight deadlines.

THE BOTTOM LINE: Look past the title and the formal organizational structure, and use effective questioning to get your contact to identify the person who has the *actual* power to make things happen for you. Then try to set a meeting with your contact *and* that person.

SKILL #24

Close the Sale

"I think I'm ready to close the deal—but I'm uncomfortable using the 'closing tricks' I've read about it in so many sales books. Any advice?"

———————

You *should* be uncomfortable with those tricks. They're manipulative, unprofessional, and ineffective.

If you've spent most of your time *gathering information*, your plan will actually *make sense* to the prospect. That means you won't need fancy closing tricks. Instead, you can simply say: "It makes sense to me—what do you think?"

This is the world's simplest—and most effective closing technique. This strategy assumes that you have spent most of your time gathering and verifying information about what the prospect is doing and how you can help him or her do that better.

When we use this "makes sense to me" closing strategy I've just described, we're forcing the other person to react. It's a little bit like tossing a ball out to the prospect: He or she has to respond somehow. If the person catches the ball and tosses it back to us by saying, "Yes, it does make sense; when can we start?" then we know we've closed the sale. By the same token, the other person could respond, "No, it doesn't make sense." Then we can ask, "Really? Why not?" At that point, more often than not, we're going to learn *exactly* what is standing in the way of our doing business together.

And that's the key point to remember. When people tell us why our suggested proposal *doesn't* make sense, they are actually telling us what is wrong and how to correct it. The relationship is still moving forward. We've been "righted."

THE BOTTOM LINE: Use the closing technique described in this chapter. Be sure you precede the request by gathering and verifying information about what the prospect is doing and how you can help him or her do that better.

Avoid the Ten Most Common Mistakes

"I'm a manager training a new sales team. What are the most common mistakes salespeople make? And how can I help my people avoid them?"

——————

You could do worse than sharing the following list of common errors—and their parallel success strategies. The ten observations that follow are based on my twenty-seven years of experience in sales and my company's interactions with nearly half a million sales reps.

MISTAKE #1

Not setting up the next appointment during the first meeting. Asking for the meeting while you're still face to face with the prospect will accelerate your sales cycle. Don't walk into a meeting with a prospect without knowing what you plan to *ask* for during that meeting—and *how* you plan to ask for it.

MISTAKE #2

Not verifying your information. The best way to verify your information is with an "outline" or "preliminary proposal." See Chapter 21 for all the details.

MISTAKE #3

Not escalating the sale. Don't be afraid to bring a manager in. All too often, salespeople think it's a sign of weakness to say, "Would you be willing to meet with me and my manager next Tuesday at two o'clock?" Actually, this puts you in a position of strength! You show the prospect that you take his or her business seriously. And you show your manager that you're strategizing the sale effectively and working to move forward to the next step.

You can also escalate the sale by arranging for the prospect to meet with your technical or creative people or with an important third party, such as another vendor or an accountant.

MISTAKE #4

Ignoring what makes this customer unique.
Don't assume that this customer is the same as
the last one. Don't get distracted by what you
think the person needs. Ask do-based questions to find out what makes this person and
this organization different. For instance:
"What do you do here? How long have you
been with the company? How did you get this
job? What are you trying to get accomplished
this quarter? What kind of customers are you
trying to attract? Who are your key vendors?
Who do you consider your most important
competitor? How did you do this last time?
What made you pick that company? What do
you want to see happen as a result of this program?" There are literally hundreds of varia-
tions on this "do-based" questioning that you
can use to find out what makes *this* prospect
unique. Use them!

MISTAKE #5

Not planning two weeks in advance.
Projections get less accurate the further into the
future they go. Use your calendar as a tool to
get as specific as you possibly can about what's
going to happen in the near term—preferably
before lunch! Know what you can realistically
expect to accomplish, create, and earn over the

next fourteen calendar days. That's the critical time period, the one that really counts.

By the same token, you should take commitments from other people more seriously when they occupy this two-week window than when they don't. After all, which appointment is more likely to happen—the one I set with you for tomorrow morning at ten o'clock or the one I set with you for three months from now?

MISTAKE #6

Fixating on "yes" answers. Don't just count the "yes" answers! You have to have "no" responses if you want to generate "yes" answers. Anytime a salesperson tells me that a whole week went by without anyone saying "no," I know there's a problem.

Similarly, you have to be willing to get *corrected* in order to be correct during the sales process. Now think about that. What does that mean? It means that if you assume that you are always right and you already know everything there is to know about the prospect, you're not really learning anything during the information gathering process!

So remember that you need a "no" in order to know. If no one ever corrects you or tells you something doesn't work, that means the quality of your information is poor. Be willing to be corrected.

MISTAKE #7

Walking away without asking for specific action. Many salespeople say they are afraid of coming across as being too bossy. What they really mean is that they are afraid to ask politely and clearly for a *next step*. That's not *bossy*. That's *professional*. That's what salespeople *do*.

You have to ask the other person to do something. Otherwise you have no idea who's actually a prospect and who isn't. So ask! Ask them to schedule a meeting, take a call, meet with your boss—anything!

For instance: How many hundreds of times have you heard someone say over the phone, "Just send me some information." We suggest that salespeople say, "I prefer not to send information—let's just get together instead. How's Tuesday at two o'clock?" That's asking the prospect to *do* something. Recently, someone we were training was a little bit skeptical about this approach. But he agreed to try it. He picked up the phone. His contact said, "Send me some information." Without really thinking, he said, "Gee, I really prefer not to do that. Let's get together instead. How's Tuesday at two o'clock?" Because that's what his trainer had said during training—Tuesday at two o'clock.

The contact thought for a minute and said, "Okay. Tuesday at two o'clock it is." Well, the salesperson was not expecting that response. He had to say, "Hold it. Tuesday at two o'clock? I'm really sorry, I can't. I'm busy."

He had to do a little scrambling to secure that appointment—but at least he proved to himself how effective it is to *ask the person to do something!*

MISTAKE #8

Attempting to close when you don't know what the prospect really thinks of your plan. The whole idea behind a presentation or plan is that you think you can help the person do what he or she does better. If you have any doubts, step back and get more information!

Throughout the sales process, make sure everything you're proposing next really *makes sense* to the other person. Make sure the other person knows what you plan to do as a next step. And if the prospect doesn't know what you plan to do next, don't try to do it! That means the other person must *know* you plan to come back and ask more questions. Or meet with the prospect's boss. Or deliver a preliminary proposal. Or give your formal plan and ask for the business.

When in doubt, *say what you plan to do next* and see what happens.

MISTAKE #9
Not asking yourself intelligent questions. Never stop asking yourself, "What do I do if something goes wrong here?" Ask yourself, "What could make this sale go wrong?" Ask yourself, "What could happen to throw my income projection off—and what can I do to hit my goals anyway?"

Don't just rely on the best-case scenario. Play your scenarios forward. Play your scenarios backward. Figure out your backup plan.

Let's say you've got a prospect that looks good now. Ask yourself, "What does my income picture look like if that prospect falls through the cracks?" It happens!

Develop a fallback position for your prospect base as a whole by making sure you have enough prospects and enough first appointments. Develop a fallback plan within individual accounts by figuring out a *second* reason for coming back for another meeting—just in case the first one doesn't work out.

MISTAKE #10

Relying too heavily on technology. It's true. Even in the twenty-first century, superior salespeople actually show up. They look the person in the eye. They don't get distracted by all our fancy communications technology. Don't get me wrong. They use the technology—but they use it to support face-to-face human relationships.

Fax machines are great. Computers are great. E-mail is great. The Internet is great. All these things can support the sales process. But you have to be willing, at some point, to sit down across from your prospect, pull out your yellow legal pad and your pen, and ask, "What are you trying to accomplish here?"

Keep asking questions about what the person *does* and what he or she is trying to *accomplish*. Keep listening to the answers. Keep looking for ways you can help the person do what he or she does better.

If you do that, you will be successful.

THE BOTTOM LINE: Learn—and avoid—the ten most common sales mistakes.

Epilogue:
Don't Kid Yourself

And here's the twenty-sixth thing they don't teach you in sales school. It comes here in the Epilogue—but it may actually be the most important advice of all.

Don't kid yourself.

Here are six common bits of self-deception that have short-circuited too many sales careers. Don't let them short-circuit yours.

1. *"That's a good prospect."* As you've learned in this book, the only true prospect is someone who commits *specifically* to work through the sales process with you—by committing to a clear date and time. Anybody else is an *opportunity* you may want to turn into a prospect. Simply wanting to sell to someone or doing research on a company is not enough! You should

maintain a minimum number of active prospects at all times. (What that number is, of course, depends on your own selling cycle and income goals, but you could do worse than to start with twenty prospects and adjust from there based on your own experience.)

2. *"I have enough prospects for now."* We've trained hundreds of thousands of salespeople over the years. The vast majority of them have fewer active prospects than they think—and only learn the truth when they hit a fallow period. Unfortunately, it usually takes them weeks or months to build the base of new prospects back up to an optimal level. That's usually a painful period in terms of personal income. It doesn't have to be, though. Prospect daily—and be sure you hit daily targets that support your sales goals.

3. *"That meeting went pretty well."* Did it? If the person didn't agree to meet or speak with you at a specific date and time, it didn't really go well at all!

4. *"I can make this person do what I want to do."* There is nothing you can do to make someone do something he or she does not believe to be in his or her best

interests. The key to success in sales lies not in interpersonal manipulation but in getting in front of enough people and asking enough intelligent questions to get a critical percentage of them to act when you make a recommendation based on what you've heard. Thousands of years ago, Lao Tzu wrote in the *Tao Te Ching* that "Gentleness overcomes rigidity." In terms of selling in the twenty-first century, a good translation might be, "You only get to lead after you've demonstrated, by asking and listening, that you are focused on helping the people do what they do better."

5. *"I should be able to close this."* The use of conditional language ("should," "ought," "might") in reference to accounts that you hope to close should be a tip-off that there's a problem somewhere. Why is there any doubt? Does the person *know* you intend to close the sale? If the prospect doesn't want the sale to happen as much as you do, don't count on it!

6. *"I've got this job down."* Even the most seasoned, most experienced person can go from hero to zero with

alarming speed in today's economy. How? By neglecting personal and professional development. This is the kind of job you never really "get down." Keep learning. Keep growing. Keep asking, "How can I do this better?" Keep listening to the answers you hear.

Good luck!
Stephan Schiffman

Also by Stephan Schiffman:

*25 Sales Strategies
That Will Boost Your Sales Today!*

Trade paperback, 128 pages
$6.95, 1-58062-116-3

"Nobody who knows sales can deny the truth of Steve's simple yet profound ideas."
—Lyn Yanez,
Senior Business Service
Representative,
Sprint Corporation

Stephan Schiffman, America's #1 corporate sales trainer, delivers more of the simple, direct, easy-to-apply sales advice that has helped thousands of businesses around the world. He reveals 25 new sales-building strategies that he's developed and tested during his years of training top-notch salespeople. Put these effective, yet simple, strategies to work for you!

Also by Stephan Schiffman:

25 Most Common Sales Mistakes and How to Avoid Them

Trade paperback, 128 pages
$6.95, 1-55850-511-3

"Steve Schiffman is a great source of practical, real-life, results-oriented insights. You can read his books again and again."
—Patricia C. Simpson,
Vice President,
Chemical Bank

Are you losing sales you should have made? Most salespeople are! Why? They make fundamental mistakes—ranging from failing to really listen to potential clients to failing to stay in touch after a sale. Stephan Schiffman's clear, concise, easy-to-use handbook shows you how to identify and correct these costly errors.

Available wherever books are sold.

For more information, or to order, call 800-872-5627 or visit www.adamsmedia.com

Adams Media Corporation, 57 Littlefield Street, Avon, MA 02322. U.S.A.

About the Author

Stephan Schiffman is the president of D.E.I. Management Group, Inc., the fifteenth largest sales training company in the United States. He is the author of a number of bestselling books including *Cold Calling Techniques (That Really Work!), Power Sales Presentations, The 25 Most Common Sales Mistakes, The 25 Habits of Highly Successful Salespeople, Asking Questions, Winning Sales, High-Efficiency Selling,* and most recently, *Make It Happen Before Lunch*. Mr. Schiffman's articles have appeared in many publications including the *Wall Street Journal,* the *New York Times,* and *INC. Magazine.* He has also appeared as a guest on CNBC's *Minding Your Business, How to Succeed in Business, Smart Money,* and TCI's *Arlington Business Today.* For more information about Schiffman and D.E.I. Management, please call (212) 581-7390, or visit our Web site at *www.dei-sales.com.*